PORTRAIT OF HONG KONG

Published by
The Hamlyn Publishing
Group Limited
London/New York
Sydney/Toronto

Hamlyn House, Feltham,
Middlesex, England

© Copyright
The Hamlyn Publishing
Group Limited 1970

ISBN 0 600 01786 9

Printed in Hong Kong
by Lee Fung
Printing Company Ltd.

PORTRAIT OF
HONG KONG
PHOTOGRAPHS
BY EDWARD
SMART
INTRODUCTION
BY SIR ROBERT
BLACK
GCMG OBE

PAUL HAMLYN
LONDON/NEW YORK
SYDNEY/TORONTO

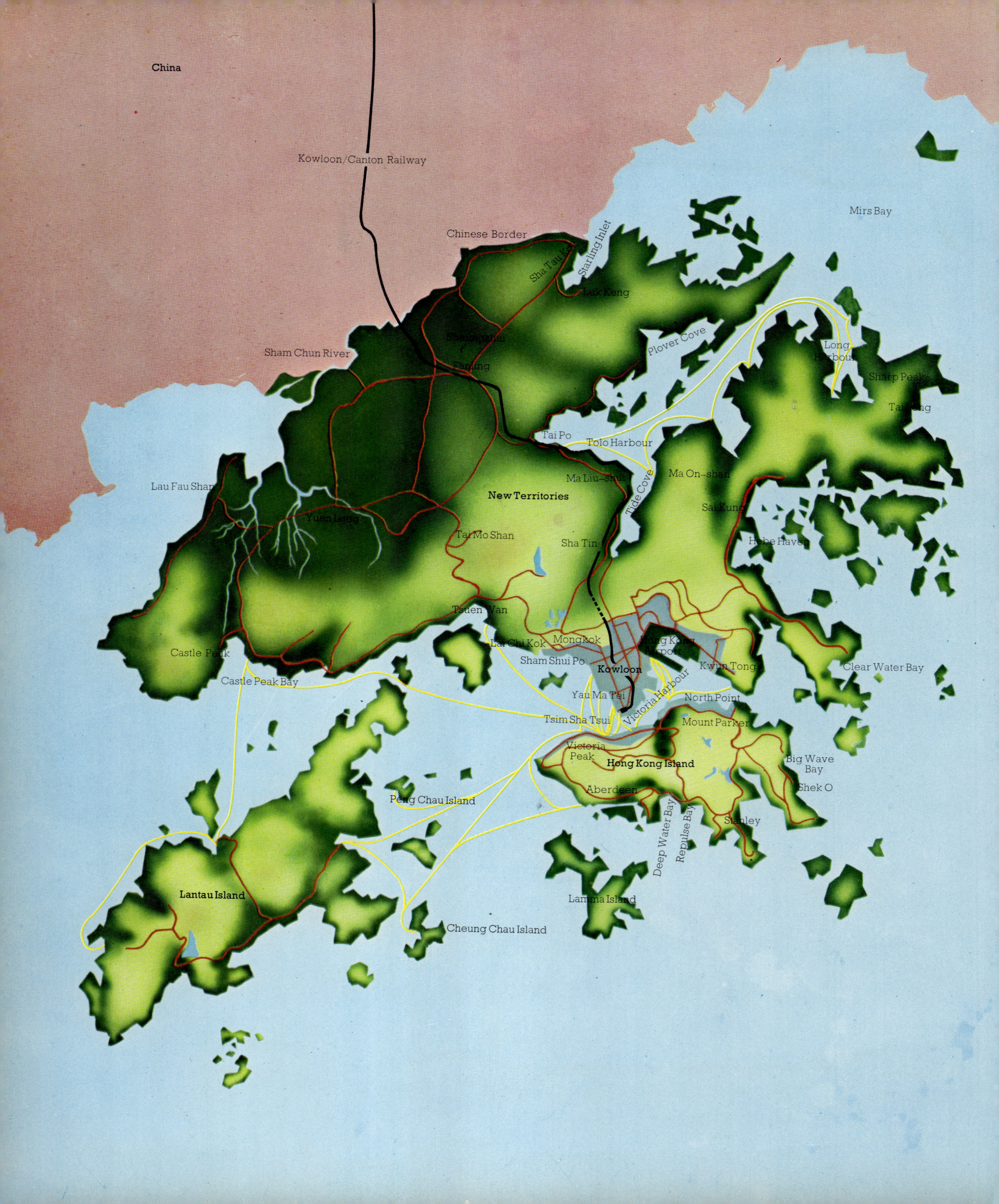
China
Kowloon/Canton Railway
Mirs Bay
Chinese Border
Starling Inlet
Sha Tau Kok
Luk Keng
Plover Cove
Sham Chun River
Fanling
Long Harbour
Sharp Peak
Tai Po
Tolo Harbour
Lau Fau Shan
Ma Liu-shui
Tide Cove
Ma On-shan
Sai Kung
New Territories
Yuen Long
Tai Mo Shan
Sha Tin
Hebe Haven
Tsuen Wan
Lai Chi Kok
Mongkok
Hong Kong Airport
Castle Peak
Sham Shui Po
Kowloon
Kwun Tong
Clear Water Bay
Castle Peak Bay
Yau Ma Tei
Victoria Harbour
North Point
Tsim Sha Tsui
Mount Parker
Victoria Peak
Hong Kong Island
Big Wave Bay
Shek O
Aberdeen
Peng Chau Island
Deep Water Bay
Repulse Bay
Stanley
Lantau Island
Lamma Island
Cheung Chau Island

Within its frame of hills and sea, Hong Kong is a fascinating landscape. There is something in the light, there is something in the atmosphere which tempts you to take out your camera ; and, of course, there are subjects which are rewarding material for the artist, for the man concerned with human appeal, for the man interested in chronicling human achievements. Hong Kong is a treasure house for the photographer, and any visitor who sets out on foot to see all he can must be struck by the great number of young Chinese roaming around armed with cameras of all shapes and sizes and not infrequently loaded with the extra paraphernalia of the expert.

My own memories of Hong Kong are more than visual, for they are anchored to the friendships cemented while I worked there, to the associations formed while coping with the Colony's unique problems ; and, above all, is my admiration for the spirit of its people. But, in my recollections, certain pictures do recur : of chosen places and of things which happened while my wife and I lived there.

I cannot think of Hong Kong without a feeling of nostalgic affection, yet I hesitate to recite in detail the reasons for this. A diamond has its facets, but it is the whole stone which one admires. And so it is with Hong Kong. One comes to love it for the sum of its features, despite the flaws which are a consequence of the encounters to which it is exposed. Pre-eminently, there are the people with their tireless resource and their fortitude, so manifest as they make the most of an infinitesimal area of land. They have built two great cities, are well embarked on a third, and have other towns planned for development and expansion. Too many people in too small a space, with practically no natural resources : this means that life is hard and they have to be tenacious in spirit to survive ; they have to be self-reliant and, at the same time, to recognize the contingent responsibility for those dependent on them. And, in the post-war years, when Hong Kong's population has been swollen by an immense tide of refugees and immigrants, it has been especially important to encourage community co-operation in order to counter the disintegrating effects of external pressures. I have watched this co-operation develop over the years in the social services and in the economic expansion of the Colony.

Small as is the area for such a great press of people, a visitor, on approach by sea or air, gains a stirring impression of size : towering white buildings, ships at anchor in a superb harbour, guarded by a ring of hills – the high spine of Hong Kong Island from Mount Parker to Mount Austin, the heights of Kowloon, and Sunset Peak on distant Lantau. And beyond the long ridge which commands Kowloon lie the New Territories, with Tai Mo Shan in the centre, so frequently in cloud, and, to the north-east, the lovely Lam Tsun valley winding down to Tolo Harbour. This valley is rich in treasures : a high-lodged waterfall, a stream for companion most of the way, birds, wayside flowers, rhododendron and wild hibiscus shrubs, fruit trees and pleasant woods. In a sense all of this is in miniature – if you compare the scene with the immense areas of mountain and river elsewhere in the world, for instance, in neighbouring China – but it is enchanting. But for me, the loveliest part of the New Territories lies between Plover Cove and Starling Inlet, dominated by the Pat Sin Range which stretches east to Mirs Bay and, on its northern slopes, faced by China Mountain just across the frontier. Some of my happiest memories are of setting out, on a Sunday morning, from Fanling for the village of Luk Keng, and, from there, scrambling up to the long ridge marked along its length by hillocks (there are eight of them, hence 'Pat Sin', the eight fairies, a possible reference to the eight Taoist immortals). These mounds rise from the grassy ridge above an escarpment which plunges steeply down to a great cove, leading into Tolo Channel, the finger of water which points to the sea. At the eastern end one drops down through resistant, thick bamboo clumps and tearing, thorny scrub to the waterfalls of the Bride's Pool and Dragon's Pool where, in spring, rhododendrons colour the slopes bright red. The road home for me might be by the village of Chung Pui, along the shore of Plover Cove, now transformed, after ten years of planning and construction, into a great reservoir.

When we chose the site for the new Chinese University at Ma Liu-shui, near the entrance to Tide Cove, we knew how right the setting was. One would look out one day from college windows, north towards the Pat Sin and east towards Ma On-shan, the saddle-back mountain. Today, the University, on its chosen site, matches the *genius loci*.

Doubtless, not a little of the attraction of the New Territories' hills lies for me in their likeness to the mountains of Wester Ross, hills which sweep down to the sea and form the same kind of rugged promontories and enclose the same kind of lovely stretches of sand. Standing on top of Sharp Peak and looking down to the beaches of Tai Long I would be reminded of Gairloch or Gruinard Bay in the West Highlands of Scotland.

But the New Territories are not just rugged hills interspersed with lovely valleys. Placed at strategic points are lively market towns whither farmer and fisherman bring their produce : Tai Po and Yuen Long, Saikung, Sha Tin, Castle Peak, Sheungshui on the mainland, with the neighbouring islands of Peng Chau and Cheung Chau, and Sai Kwu-wan on the island of Lamma, lying athwart the great fishing centre of Aberdeen. Nature, with its rugged features, has to accept a face lift, because of the demands of a growing population for townships, factory sites, reservoirs. Nevertheless, the hills will remain, just as they do on crowded Hong Kong Island, and the cities of the Colony must lie spread in the arena below or creep up the slopes of encircling hills, while the sea acts as a girdle.

In the great cities, we leave the comparative peace of the countryside behind us with a vengeance. The roar of traffic is endless, the pavements are crowded, streams of people embark at the ferry piers on the cross-harbour boats, which ply the harbour waters all day long on established courses, threading past the large ocean-going ships which lie at anchor while lighters seem to feed on them like leeches. The cities press hard on their waterfronts, and traders mingle in unceasing passage to and from jetty and warehouse and shop. In Victoria, you may ascend the steep side-streets, leaving below you the grand buildings and stores of the business centre and fetching up at small shops where almost everything is sold. For the tourist there is one steep ascent (unless hotel car has borne him there in comfort by way of the upper levels) past a Taoist temple to Upper Lascar Road, lined with crowded junk shops where you may find furniture and chinaware, and have hopes of a ceramic bowl or a piece of jade at the end of the climb and the bargaining. In the cities you sense the tremendous vitality of the Chinese ; in pursuit of a living, they are intensely and wholly committed. It is difficult not to be infected by the energy and purposive concentration.

For all that, the noise and bustle of Hong Kong are not reserved solely for the business of making a living. One can never forget the clamour and the ritual of a Chinese New Year, with evil spirits being put to flight, the Spring Festival of Chin Ming, when thousands tend ancestral graves, the Autumn Festivals of the Mooncake and Chung Yeung, when ascent is made to the Colony's high points, and the fishermen's colourful celebrations at their temples dedicated to Tin Hau. In recent years the people of Cheung Chau have made their Bun Festival more and more spectacular, possibly with an eye on tourists as well as on evil spirits. The festivals call for elaborate organization, with due regard for tradition, and their success is usually ensured by the spirit into which they are entered both by those who take part and by those who watch.

Probably ranking with the Lunar New Year and the Autumn Festivals is the regatta of Dragon Boats. Several are held, notably in the Western District of Victoria, at Aberdeen and at Tai Po. They commemorate the suicide by drowning, in Hunan in the fourth century BC, of the scholar and statesman Chu Yuen, in protest against the State's corrupt administration. The race symbolizes the search made for his body by men in boats, armed with drums and gongs. The excitement and colour of the race, as it is energetically paddled to a finish, are heightened by the boom of the drumbeats and the appearance of the boats – a dragon's head at the bow and a dragon's tail at the stern. Banners are presented at the end of the race. In my time, a European boat was entered at Tai Po but, despite some expert guidance from the Cam, no success in the search came its way ; indeed, I recollect a watery upset and a gallant crew swimming ashore with their upturned vessel in tow.

In Hong Kong the photographic study is never 'still life'. A village, guarded by its protective To Tei shrine, when the women are threshing the rice and the men, bearing kangol-balanced buckets, are manuring their fields ; a Chinese family tomb, vault-like on a platform of stone, sited appropriately on a hillside to absorb the influences of sun and moon in accordance with the requirements of Fung Shui ; a junk in full sail, silhouetted against a setting sun ; the flats of Ping Shan at first light ; the shops and streets and high buildings in the cities – every view blends with the whole canvas of the great and continuing human achievement that is Hong Kong.

Robin Black

The life of Hong Kong begins in the harbour – historically, metaphorically and especially when the sun sets.
Cargo vessels unload their goods into fleets of lighters.

to fade. Peking Road attracts thousands of tourists shopping for watches, massages and six-hour suits.

The opening of a new night club in Kimberley Road is advertised by flower boards and a deafening flourish of fireworks.

This fruit stall in Carnarvon Road stays open until the early hours of the morning to catch customers on their way home from the bars.

The streets of Kowloon provide enough nightlife for a whole world of playboys.

The two faces of Nathan Road, night and day.

American servicemen on leave will, like most tourists, take a rickshaw ride down Nathan Road.

The day's work has begun, but the promise of evening's pleasures lingers in the flower board advertisements.

Children play in the streets outside the open Chinese shops.

17

An idle moment in the sun for the rickshaws that wait at the railway station.

Peking Road offers a glimpse of the old Hong Kong in the shadow of the new. Business is conducted in the street and washing hangs over it on bamboo poles.

The resettlement area of Ngau Taukok in the Kwan Tong factory area.

The residents of the Sau Mau Ping resettlement area lived in squatters' huts before they were rehoused by the government.

The good stone houses of Rennies Mill, stronghold of Nationalism. In this picture the Nationalist flag can be seen among those displayed at the hostel, but on 10 October it is flown from every rooftop.

A san pan, tied alongside the Kowloon public pier, bobs up and down in the wash of a larger craft.

Dockers unload freighters at Ocean Terminal. The cargo going directly onto the lighters will be taken across the harbour to Hong Kong Island.

Ocean Terminal was built to accommodate the largest of luxury liners. Passengers step off the boats into the air-conditioned heart of the largest shopping area in South-east Asia.

25

Yau Ma Tei typhoon shelter is home for almost 150,000 'boat people' who rarely set foot on land.

The Dragon Boat Races, part of one of the major festivals of the year, perpetuate the memory of an ancient scholar who drowned himself in order to awaken his king to the dangers of misrule.

The festival of the harvest moon is a great favourite with children, who light candles – and blow them out. Gaily coloured lanterns, moon cakes and prayers to the moon at night are all part of this tribute to the princess who smiles radiantly from the moon.

The birthday of the sea goddess Tin Hau is celebrated every spring by all who derive their living from the sea. Fishermen in Yau Ma Tei typhoon shelter burn hundreds of joss sticks and offer a very expensive flower board for the adornment of their patron saint.

Hong Kong's policemen, reputed to be the best in the world, have been known to handle the most serious upheavals, but are most often seen directing traffic from their pagodas.

'Nightlife' doesn't have to mean bars and clubs. In the night markets, for instance, there is plenty of life, a great deal of character and many a bargain – like these oranges from China, in the market near Maco Ferry.

This distinguished gentleman will tell your fortune.

Or you could spend one. By day this market is a car park. At night they sell jade – or cheap ceramics – between the parking meters.

Late shopping in Jordan Road, Yau Ma Tei.

Temple Street night market, often called 'the poor man's night club'.

Stalls in Temple Street offer everything from fruit to fortune-telling.

Shop and fruit stall in the back streets of Mongkok.

Rainy night in Nathan Road.

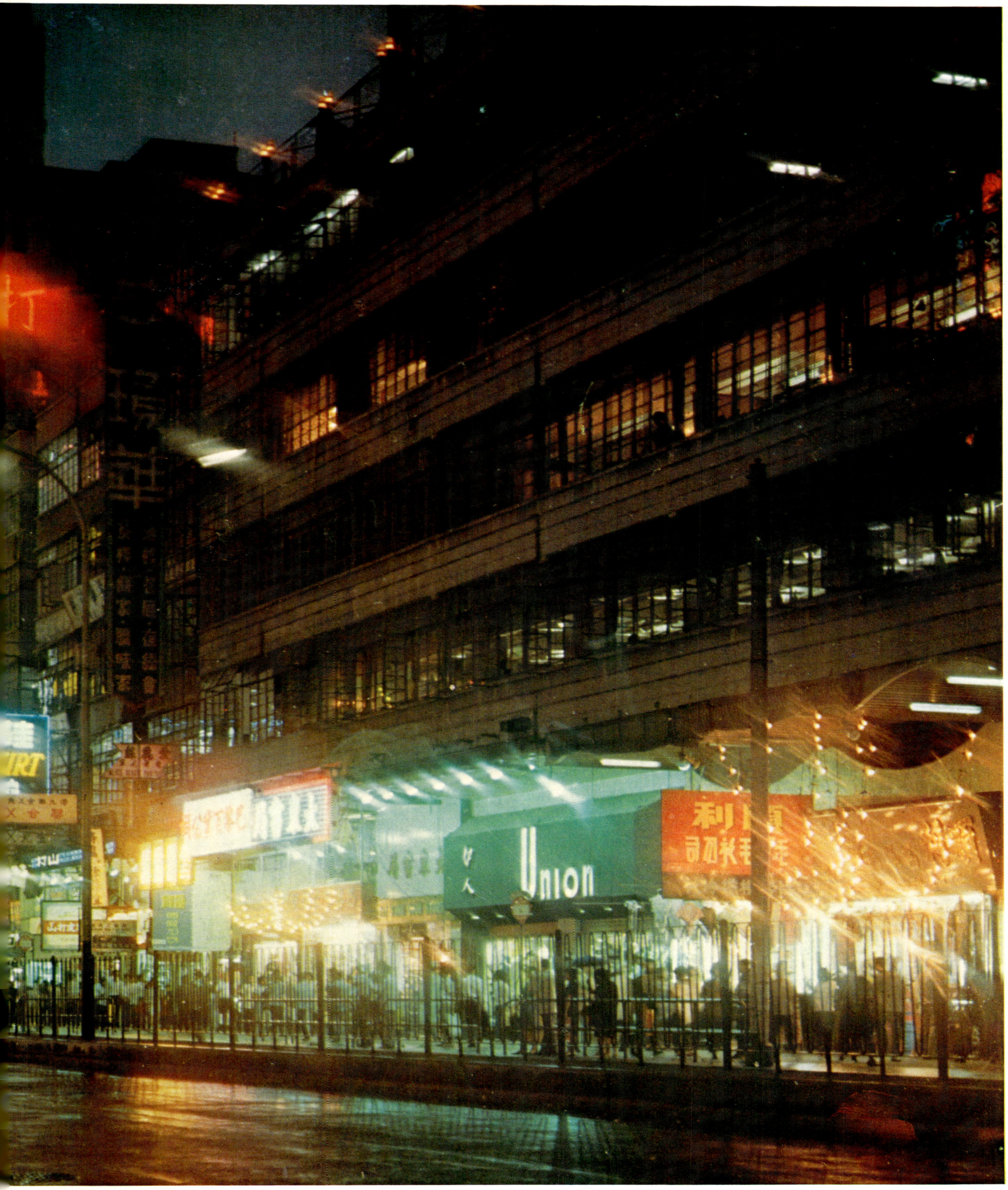
Union

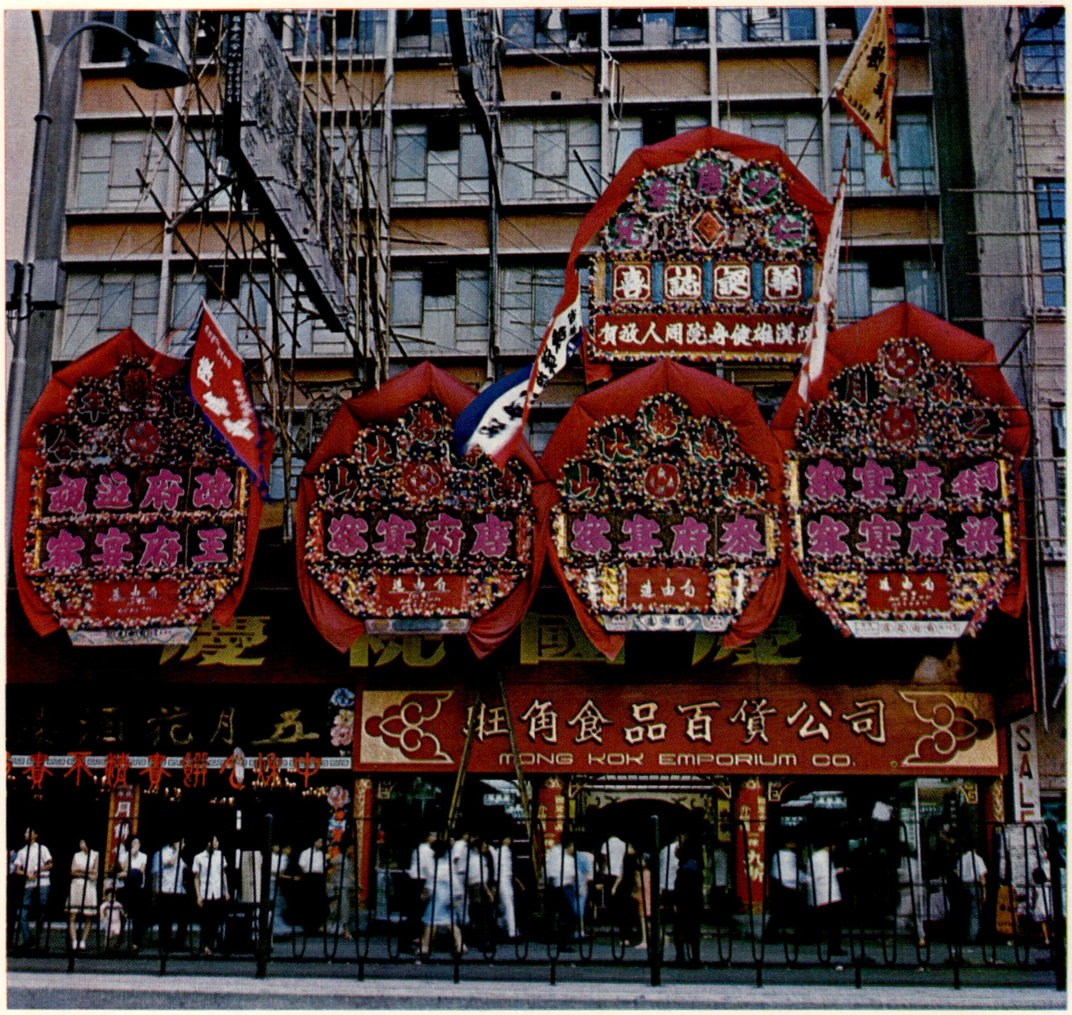
旺角食品百貨公司
MONG KOK EMPORIUM CO.

The China Emporium in Nathan Road. Flower boards and a multitude of lights herald a party.

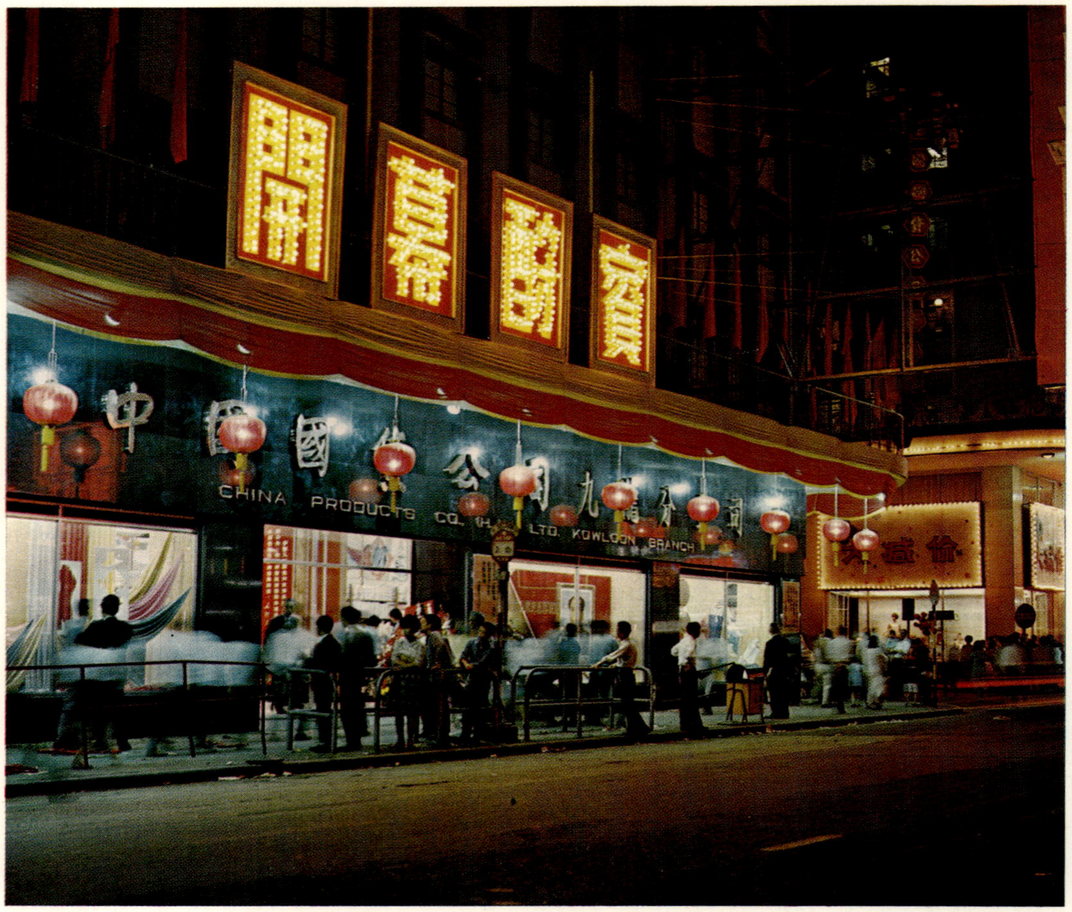
CHINA PRODUCTS CO.
LTD. KOWLOON BRANCH

The China Products Store,
Kowloon.

Gigantic billboards erected for
the October First celebrations.

Summer is long and schoolgirls wear light, short-sleeved uniforms to their Catholic school in Mongkok.

Winter is short but chilly and might even be called cold if you're waiting for a bus. The red notices advertise flats for rent.

Looking north towards Lion Rock across the skyline of Mongkok. This area is often referred to as the Concrete Jungle.

Walla walla boats chug across the harbour, supplementing the ferries. After 2 a.m. these boats are the only cross-harbour transportation.

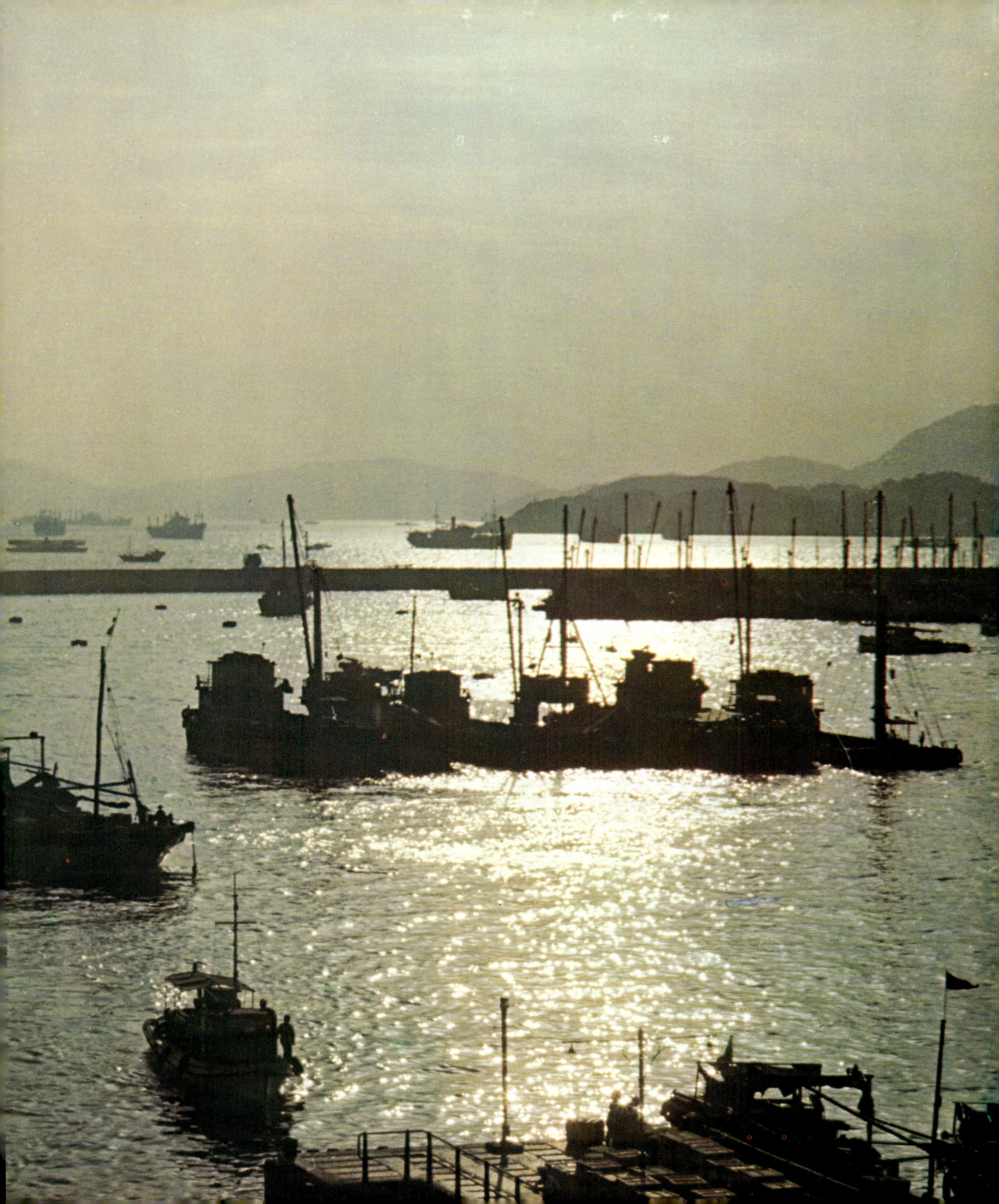

The Kwan Tong opera at the Chinese New Year festival.

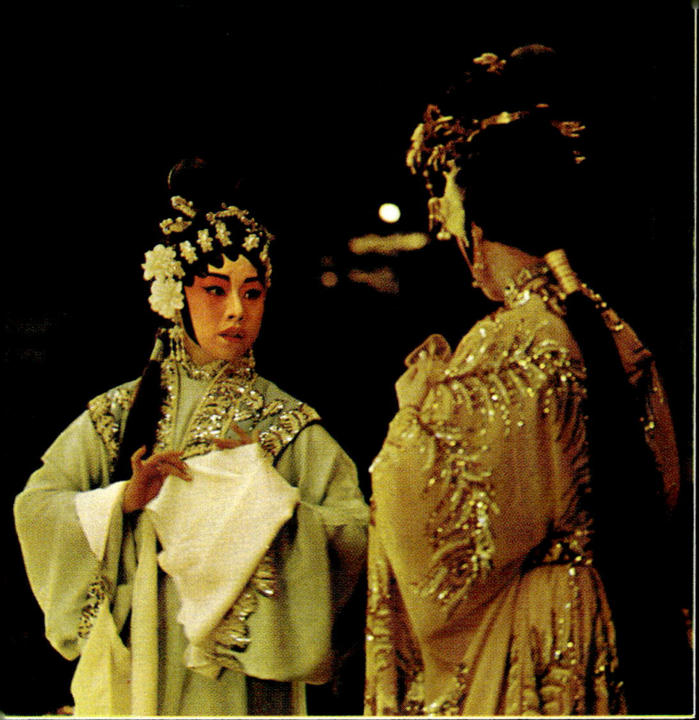

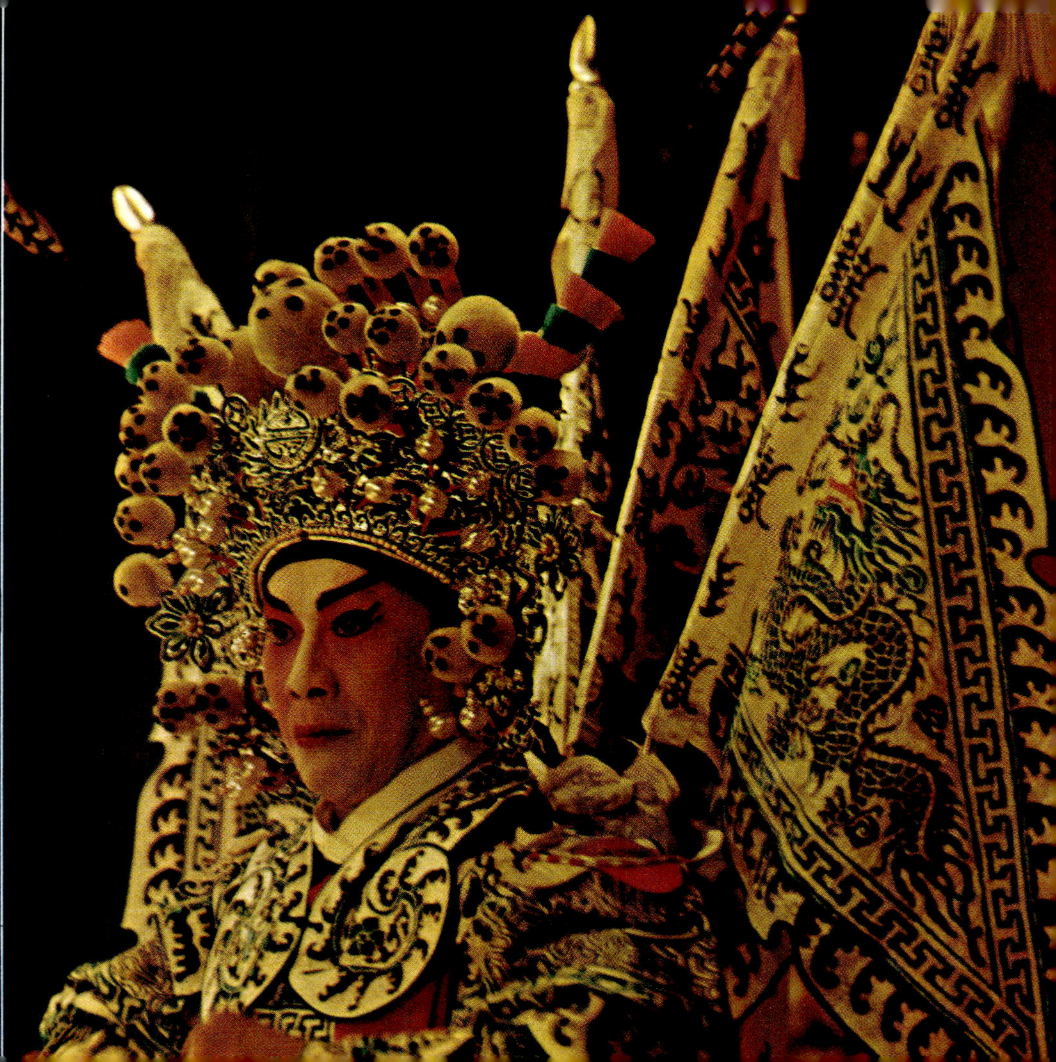

Hong Kong's famous sunsets are spectacular because of the unique combination of mountains, water, electricity and sub-tropical sun.

Victoria Peak takes on the colour of the moment. It may glow through an entire spectrum before darkness finally falls.

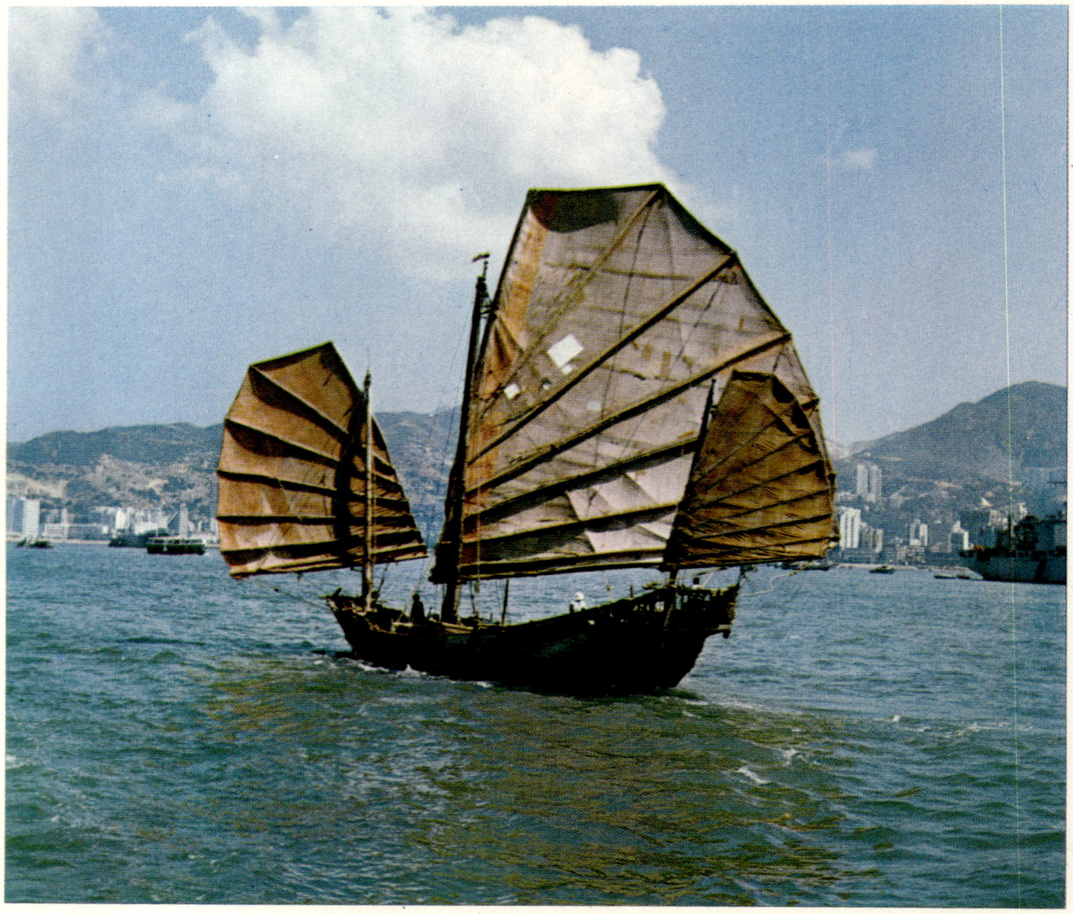

A junk without a motor is a rare thing in this modern and highly motorized harbour.

Concentrated concrete crawls up the hillside on Hong Kong Island.

The central district as seen from the ferry.

Rickshaws wait at Star Ferry.

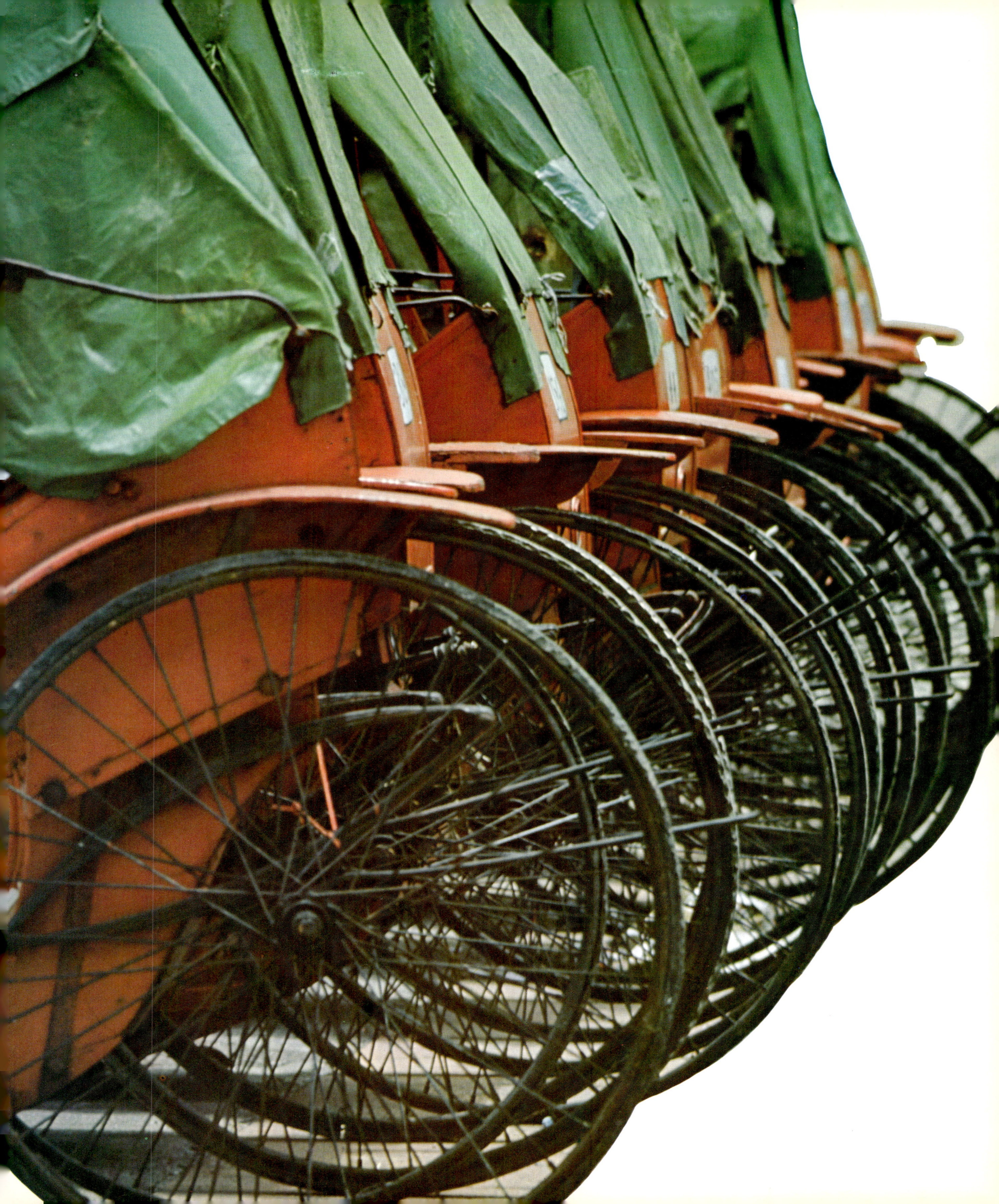

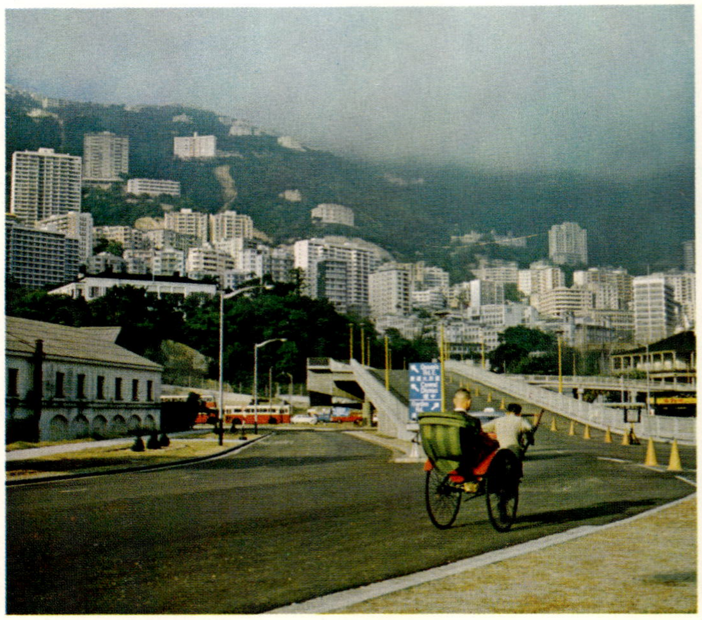

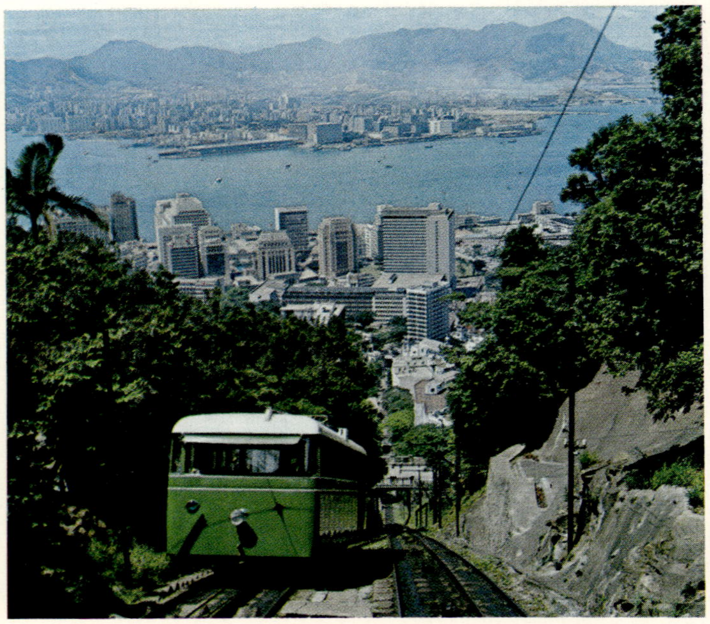

Early morning, before the heavy traffic begins.

The tram that climbs Victoria Peak leaves Hong Kong at the bottom, Kowloon and the Ocean Terminal in the background.

Harbour view from the top of Victoria Peak.

Looking east towards North Point and Causeway Bay.

Fountains in Statute Square.

Mao's portrait in a show window of the central district.

In the central district a rickshaw looks for a tourist – or a native with a heavy parcel. In the western district a boy worker takes a sugar cane break and a man unloads goods on the waterfront.

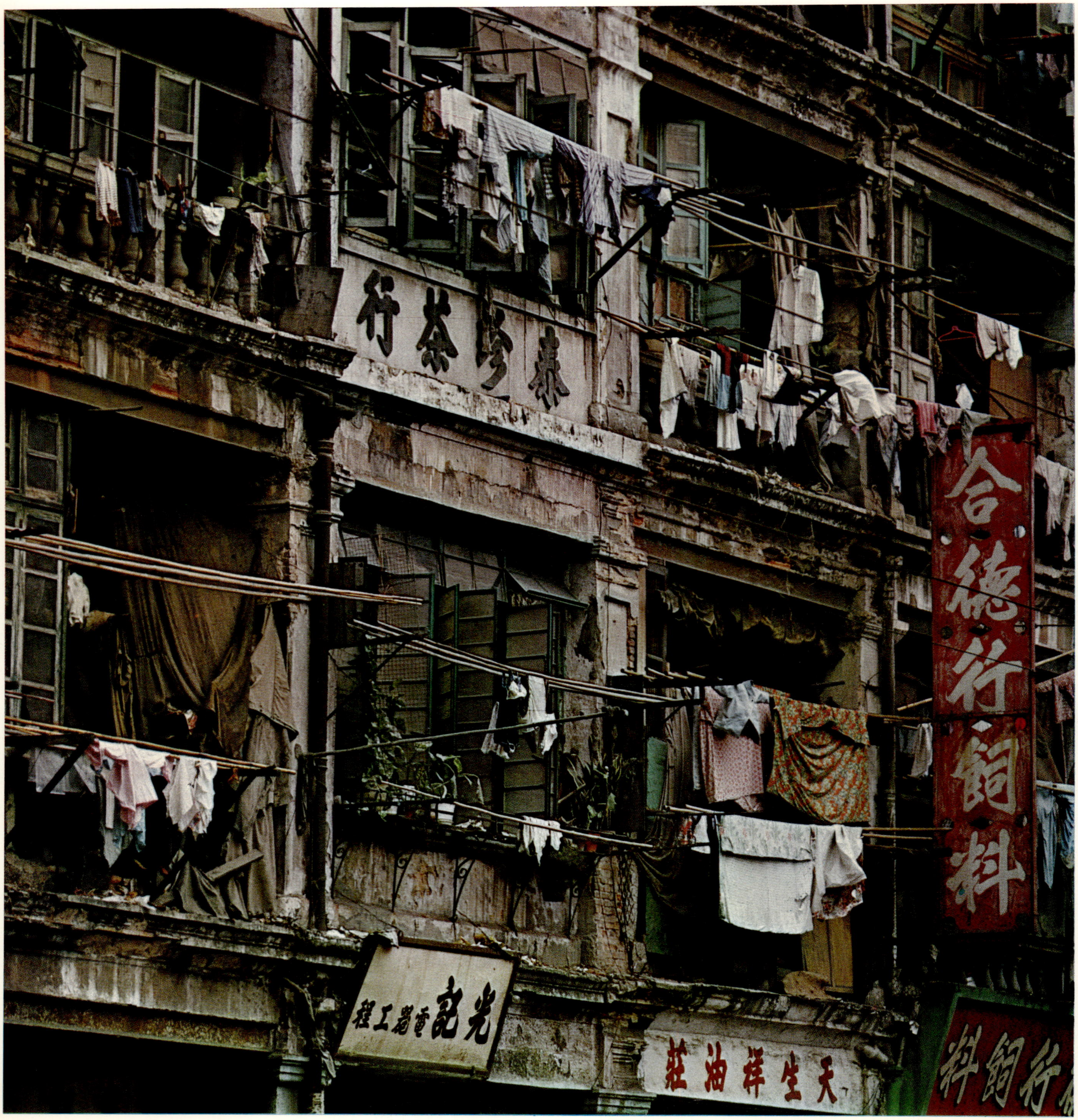
泰珍茶行
合德行飼料
光記電器工程
天生祥油莊

Signs of habitation in the western district.

Children insulated against the cold on their floating home in Causeway Bay typhoon shelter.

A tram rattles down a wide street in the western district.

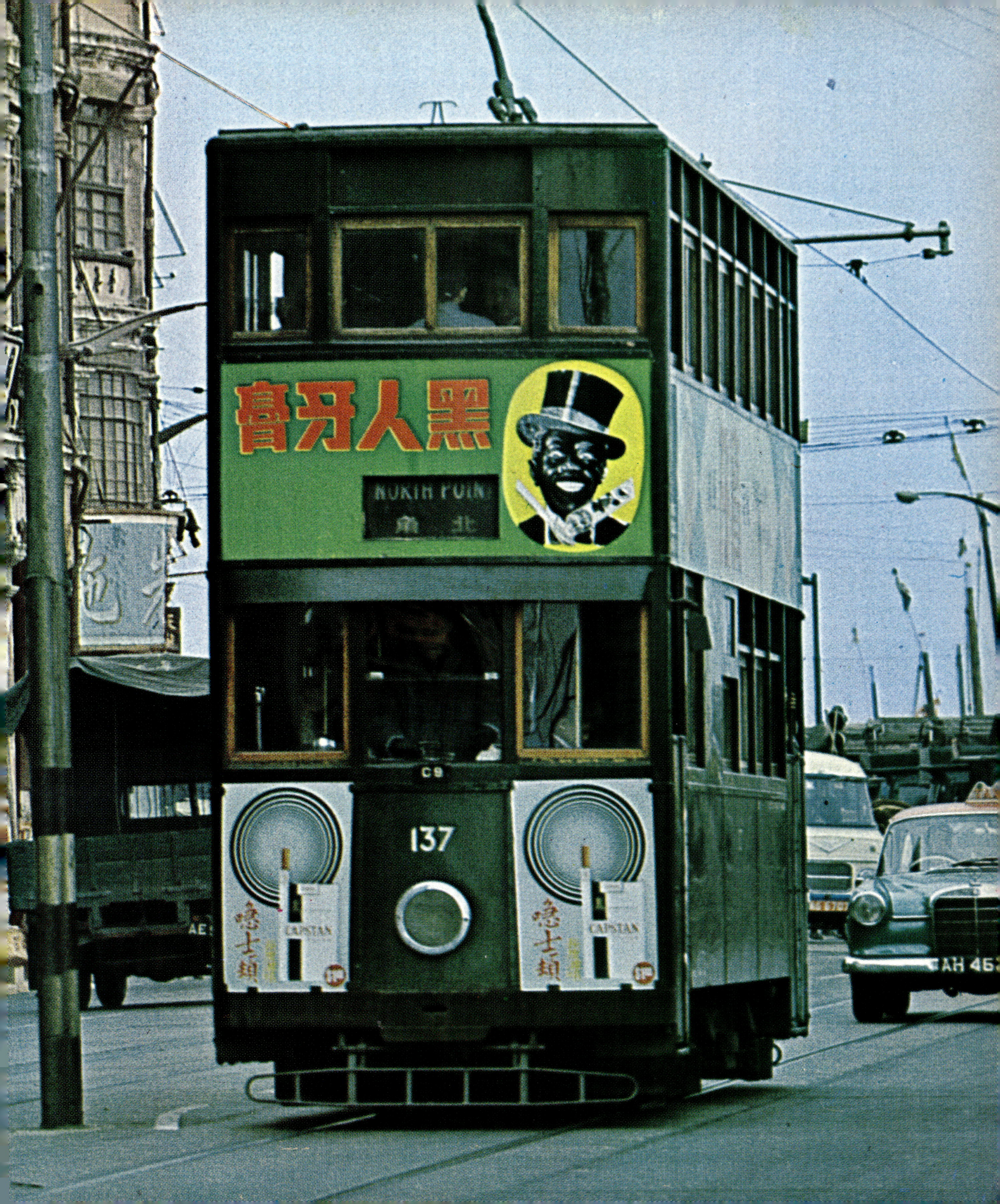

黑人牙膏
北角
C9
137
CAPSTAN
CAPSTAN

Des Voeux Road and the banking area. Trams, running in the centre of the road, unobstructed by other traffic, are still the best method of transport.

Reflections in the harbour, not of moonlight, but of mid-afternoon sun.

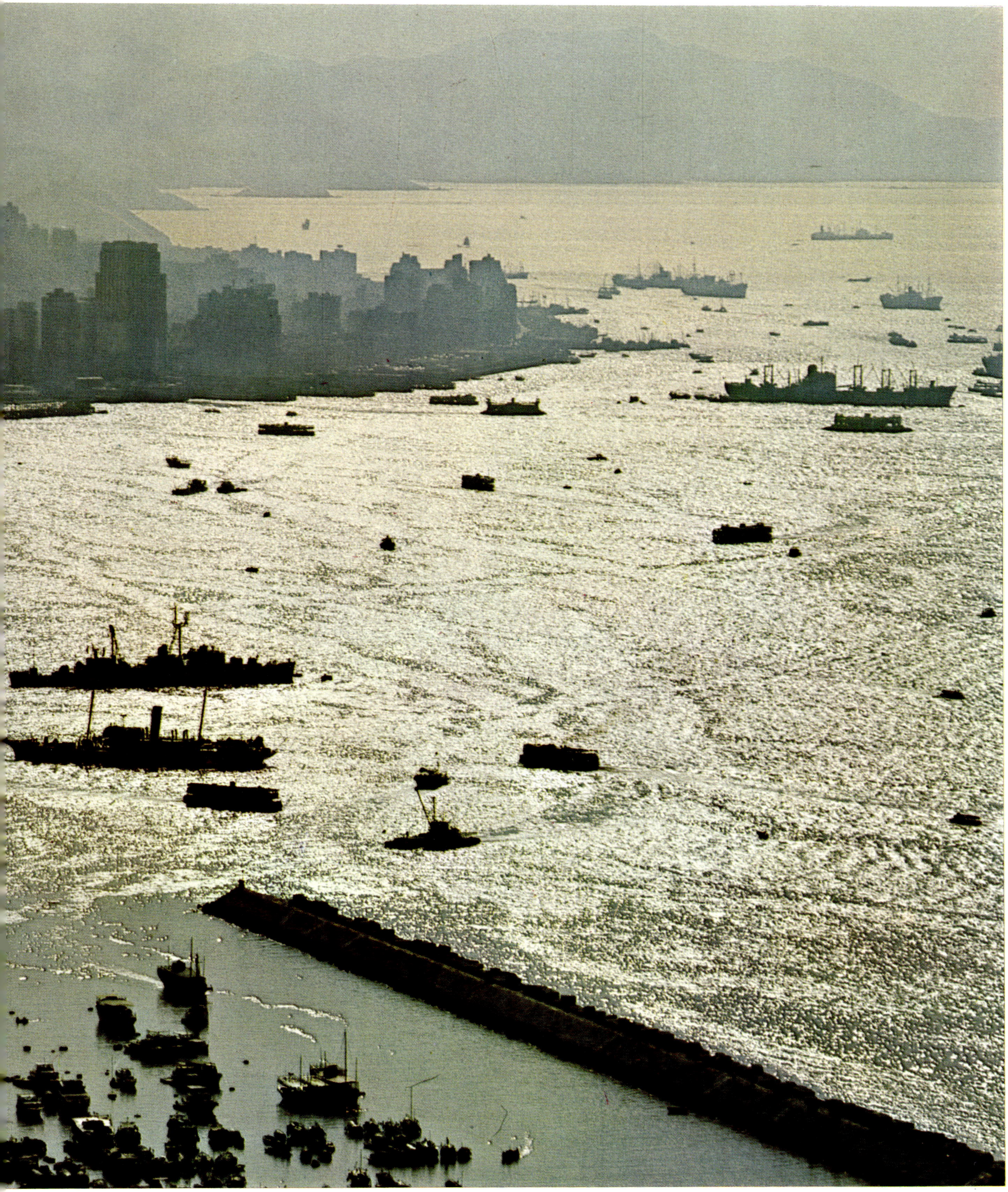

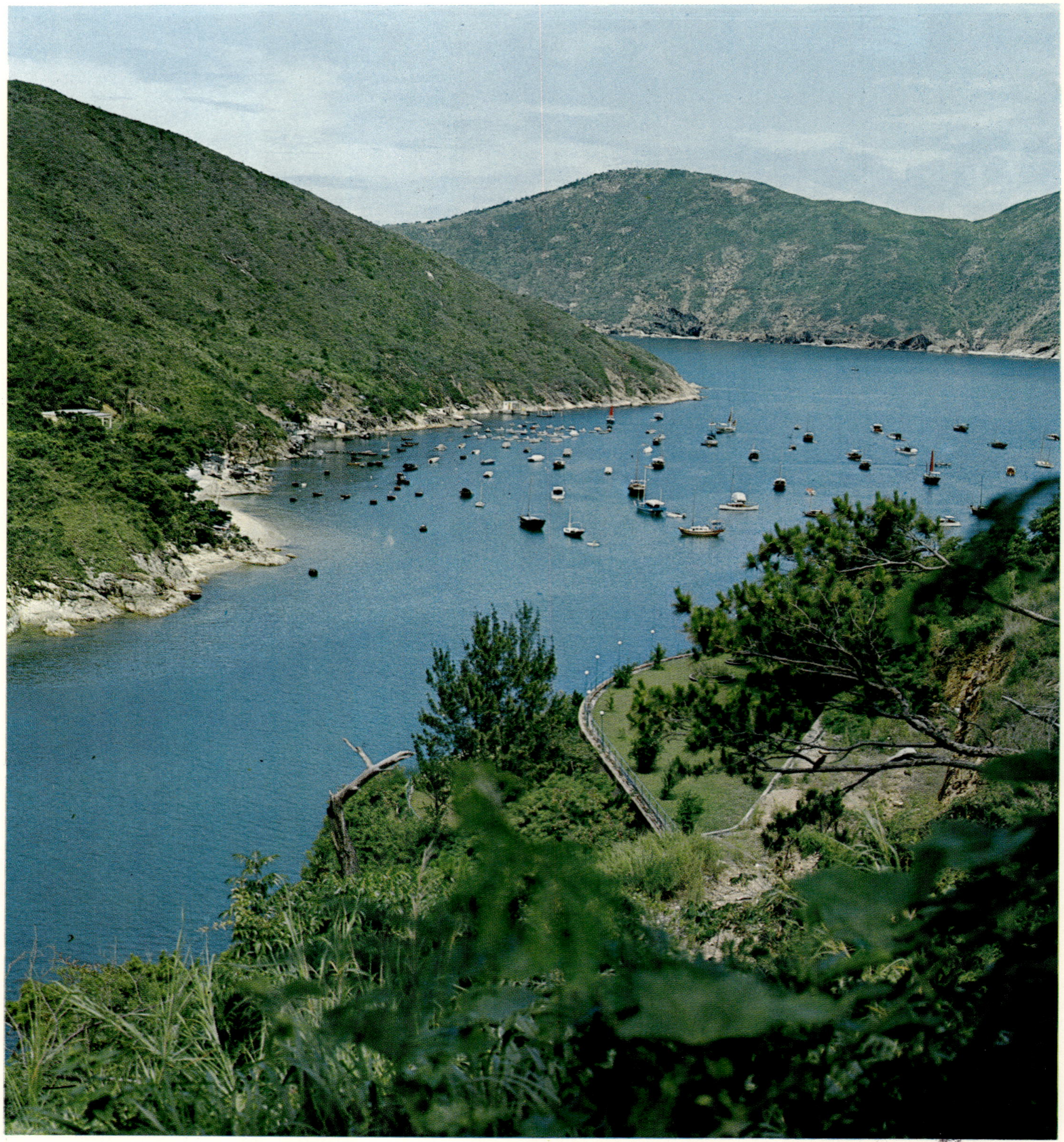

Shelter for small craft between Deepwater Bay and Repulse Bay.

Sunning on Repulse Bay Beach.

Fishing in the quiet waters between Aberdeen and Deepwater Bay.

Aberdeen, said to be the original fishing village of Hong Kong, is the home of the 'water people'. Most of these families have lived on junks for generations. The floating homes are joined together by planks, while the real travelling is done by san pan.

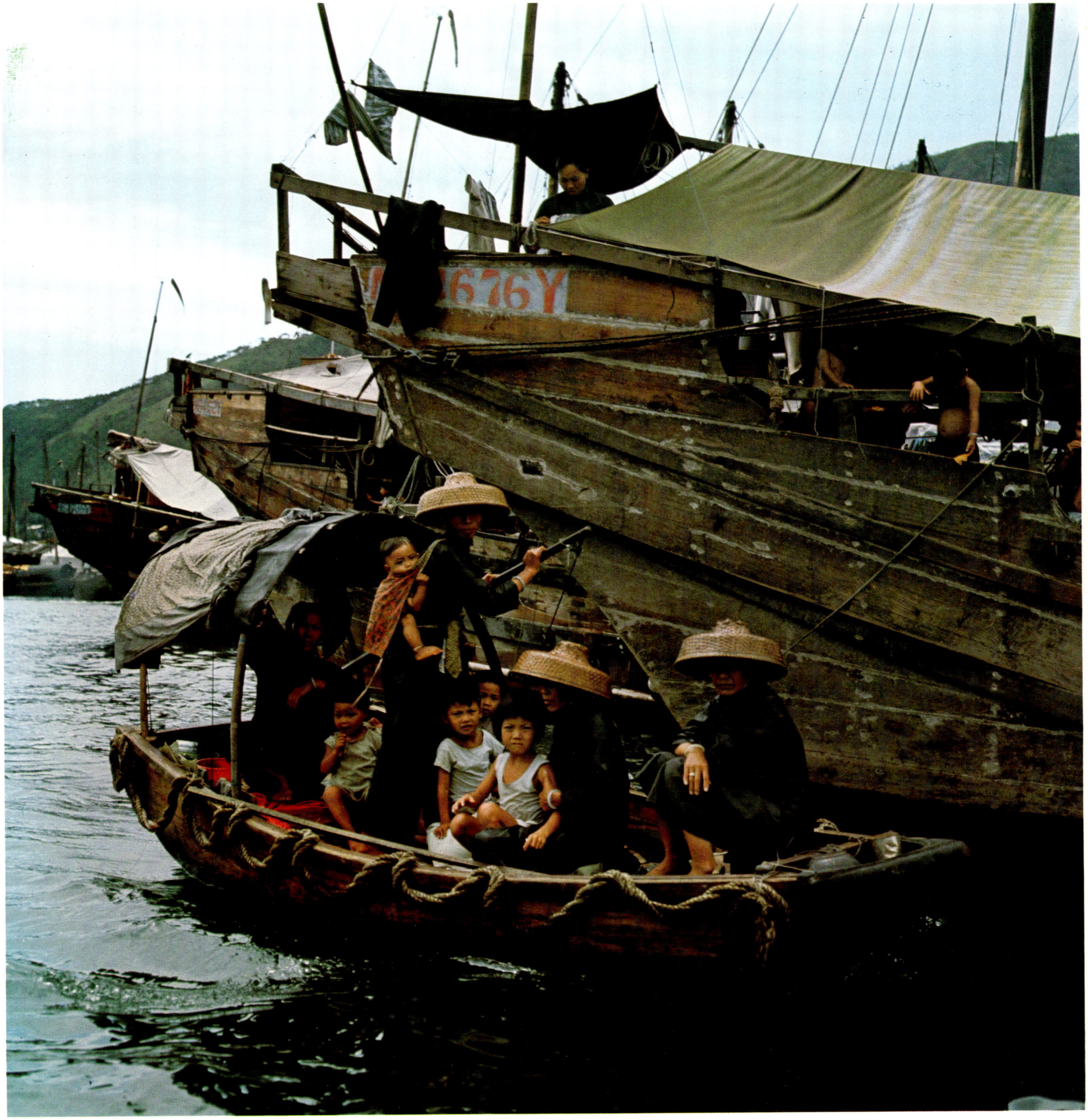
2676Y

Even a floating city has to be kept clean. This girl is collecting litter from the harbour.

Tai Pak, one of the many floating restaurants in Aberdeen.

Fisherman in wicker hat and leather jacket.

The water people on land. The main street of Aberdeen.

A street vendor with his basket full of titbits – various kinds of meat fried in batter.

When a relative dies the family burns yellow paper – a symbol of money – so that it will be received by the deceased. This ceremony is held for the first seven days after the death and then on the anniversary of the death for the next three years.

Tsuen Wan sunset from one of the small beaches.

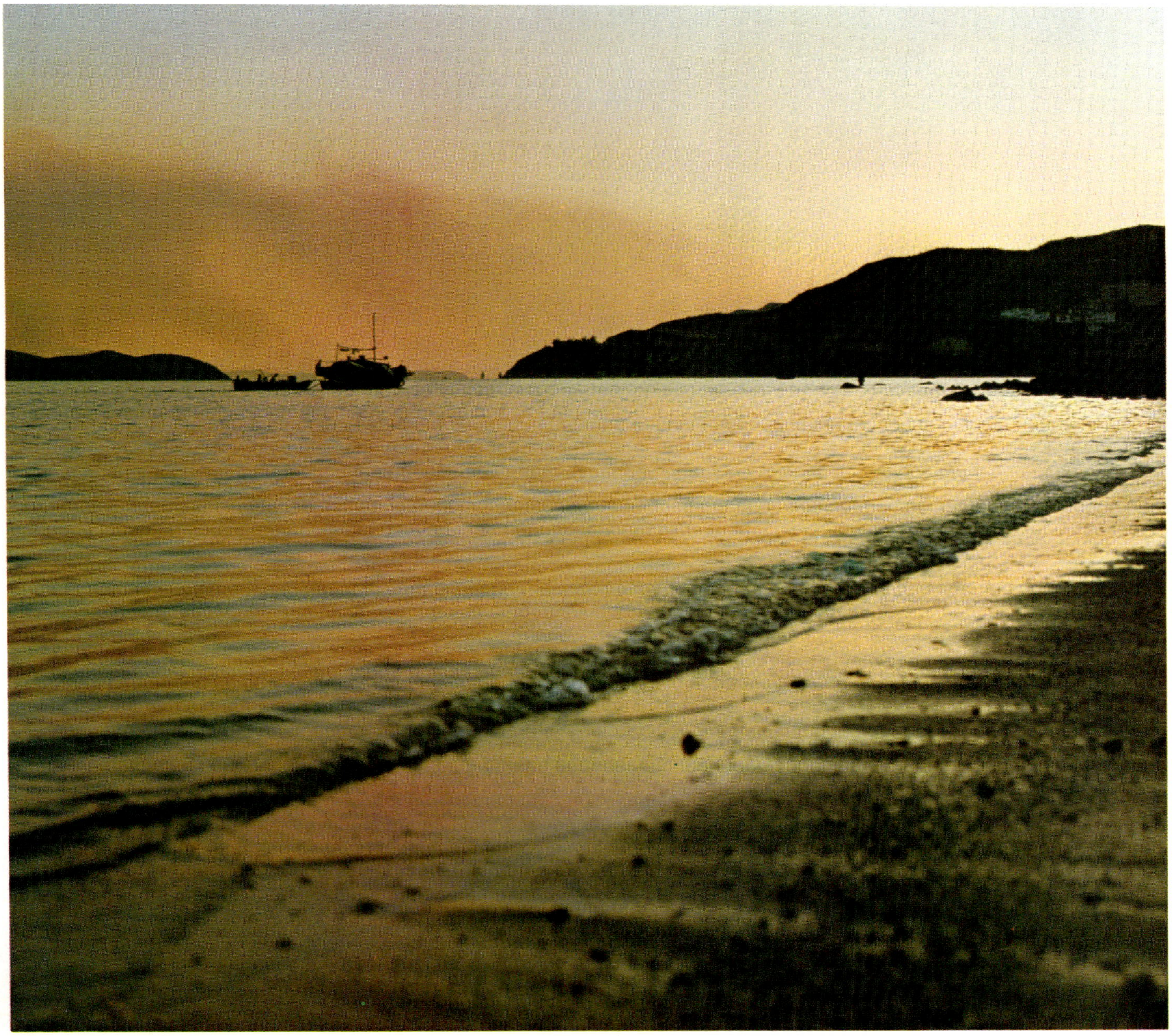

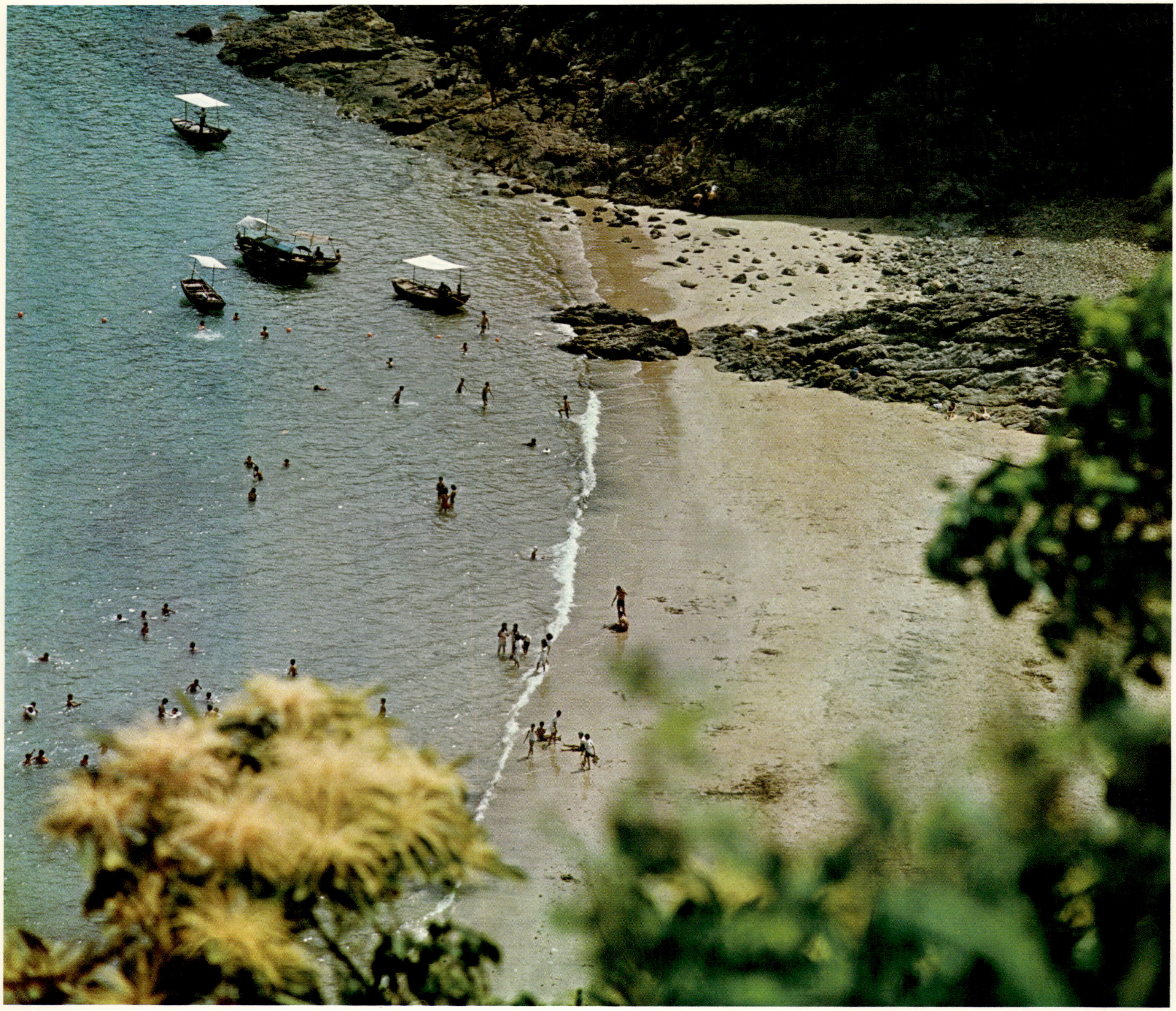

The beaches of Clear Water Bay.

Swimming off a junk anchored in the bay at Chung Chi near Ma Liu Shui.

Junks moored at Tai Po Gau. After the laundry has dried in the sunshine, they will return to their fishing grounds.

The sea is out, leaving the mud flats exposed.

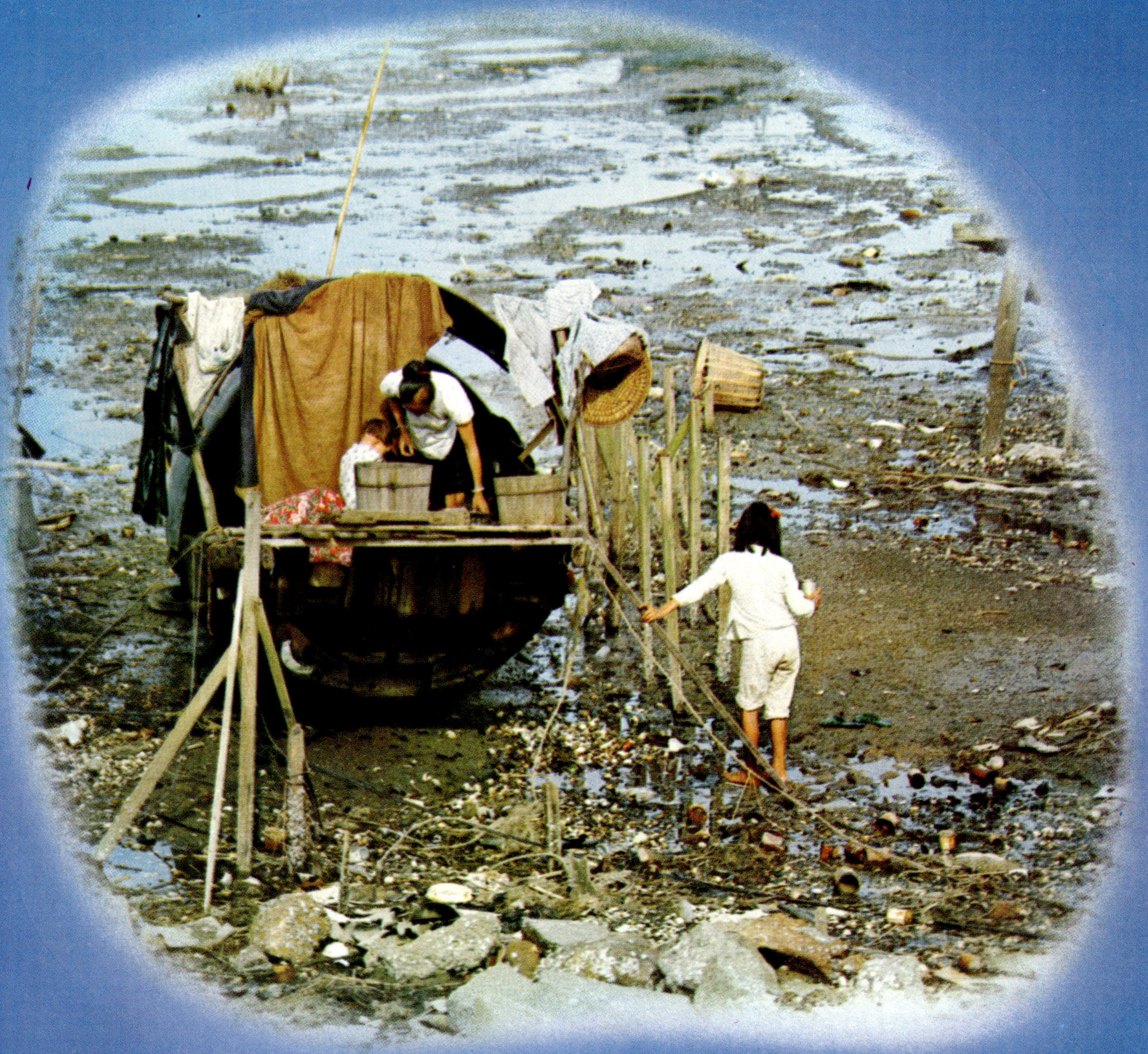

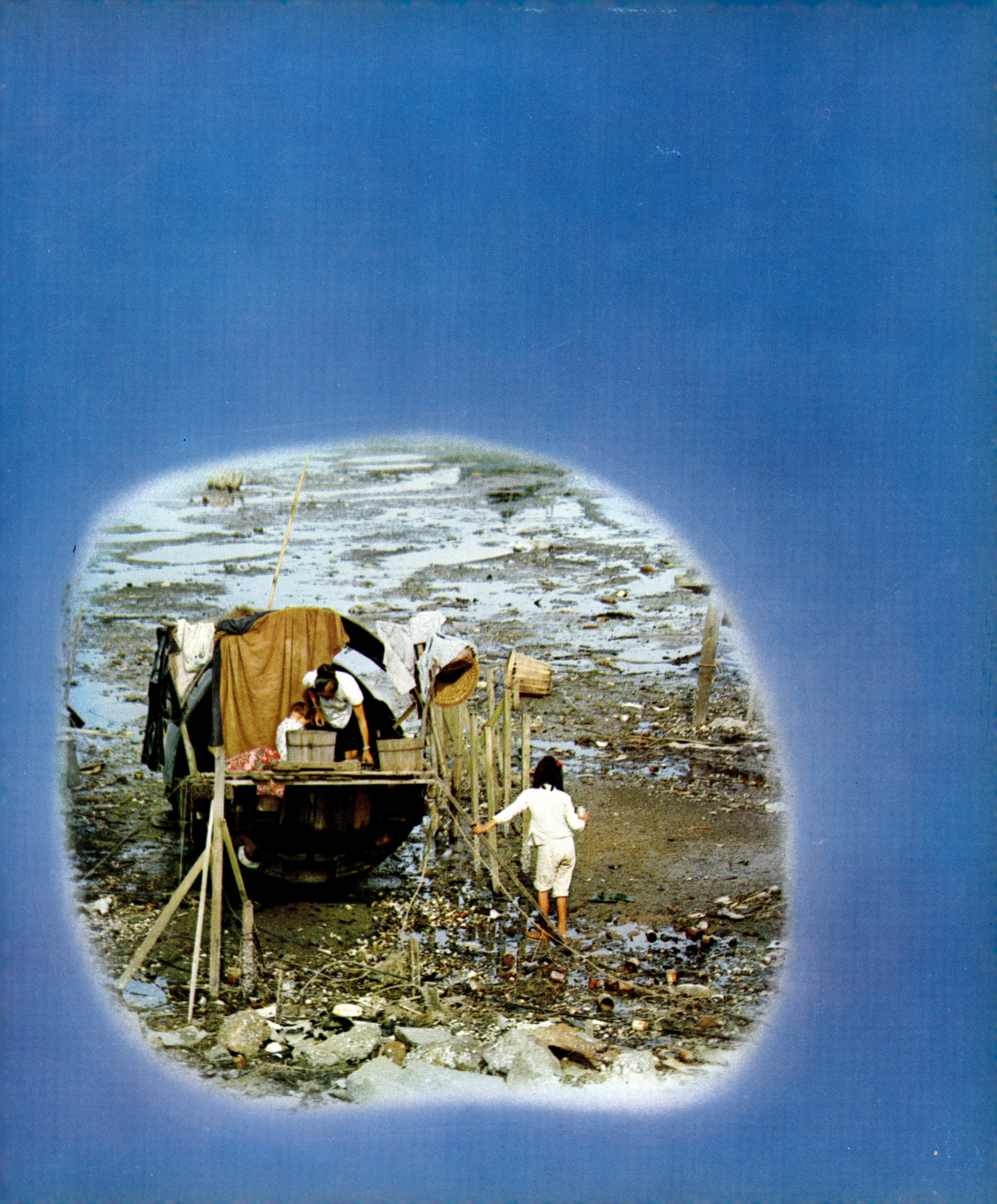

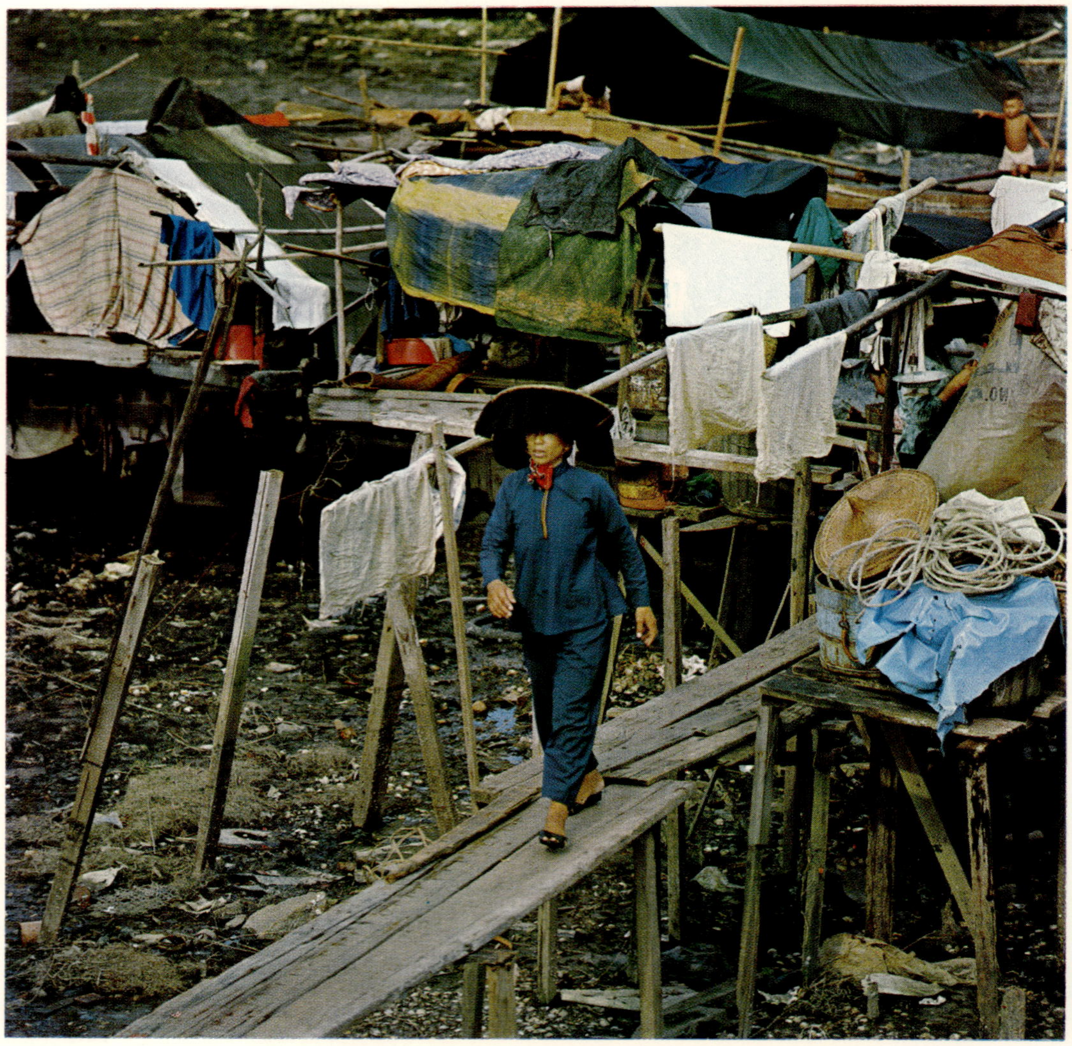

Dressed in her best outfit, a woman crosses the plank from her boat-home.

Woman worker in Sha Tin Valley. She carries two baskets of cement on a pole balanced on her shoulder blades.

Squatters' huts at the foot of Lion's Rock. The woman is carrying a child on her back and her shopping on a pole.

Children of the St Christopher's orphans' home at Tai Po.

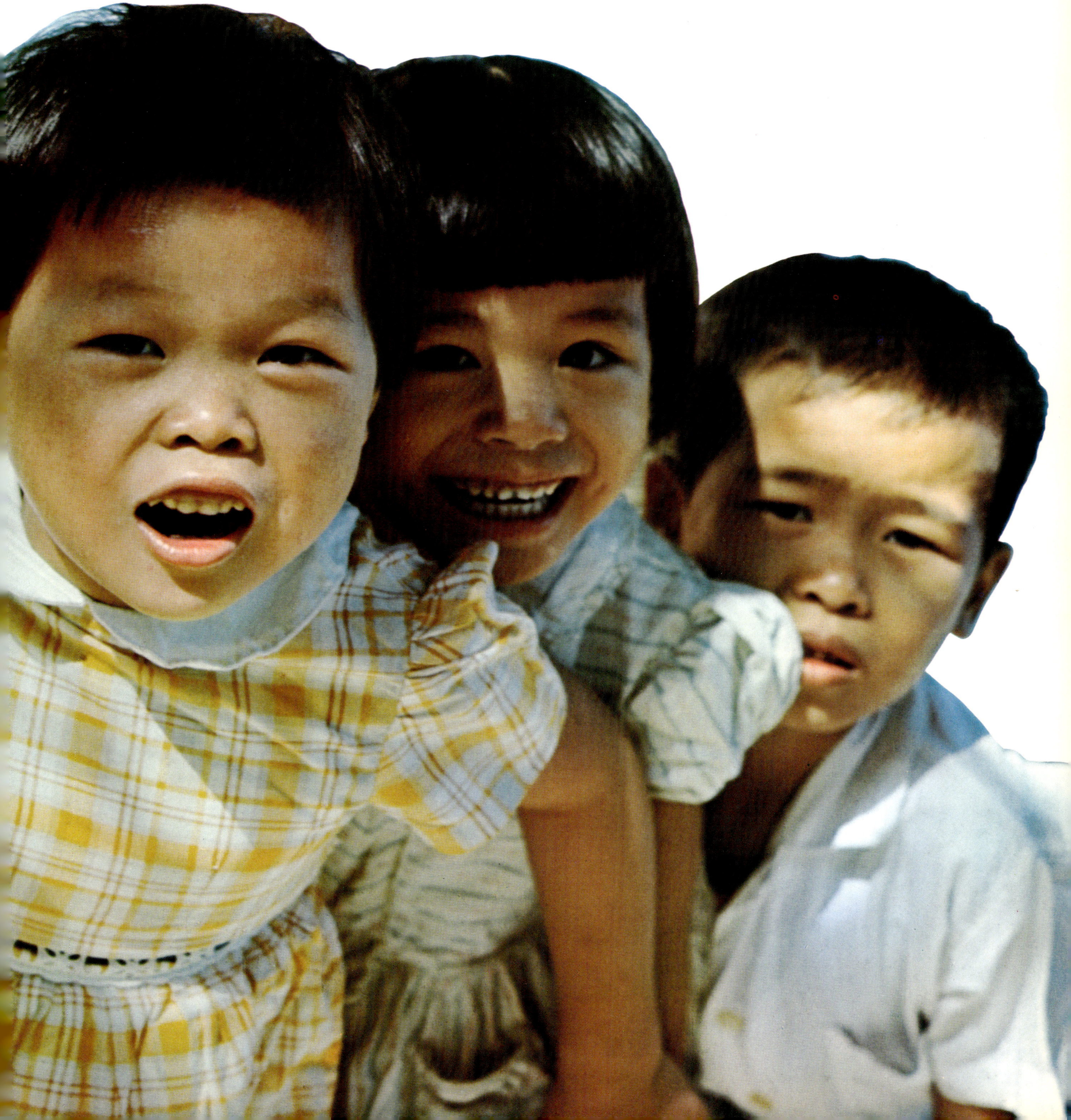

The Temple of Ten Thousand Buddhas, built about 1945, was inspired by the monk Yueb Kai, who died in 1965.

Yueb Kai was buried for eight months; his body was then exhumed and plated with gold and it now sits in the Temple of Man Fab Sha Tin.

Dying cloth and drying it on long bamboo poles in Kowloon City.

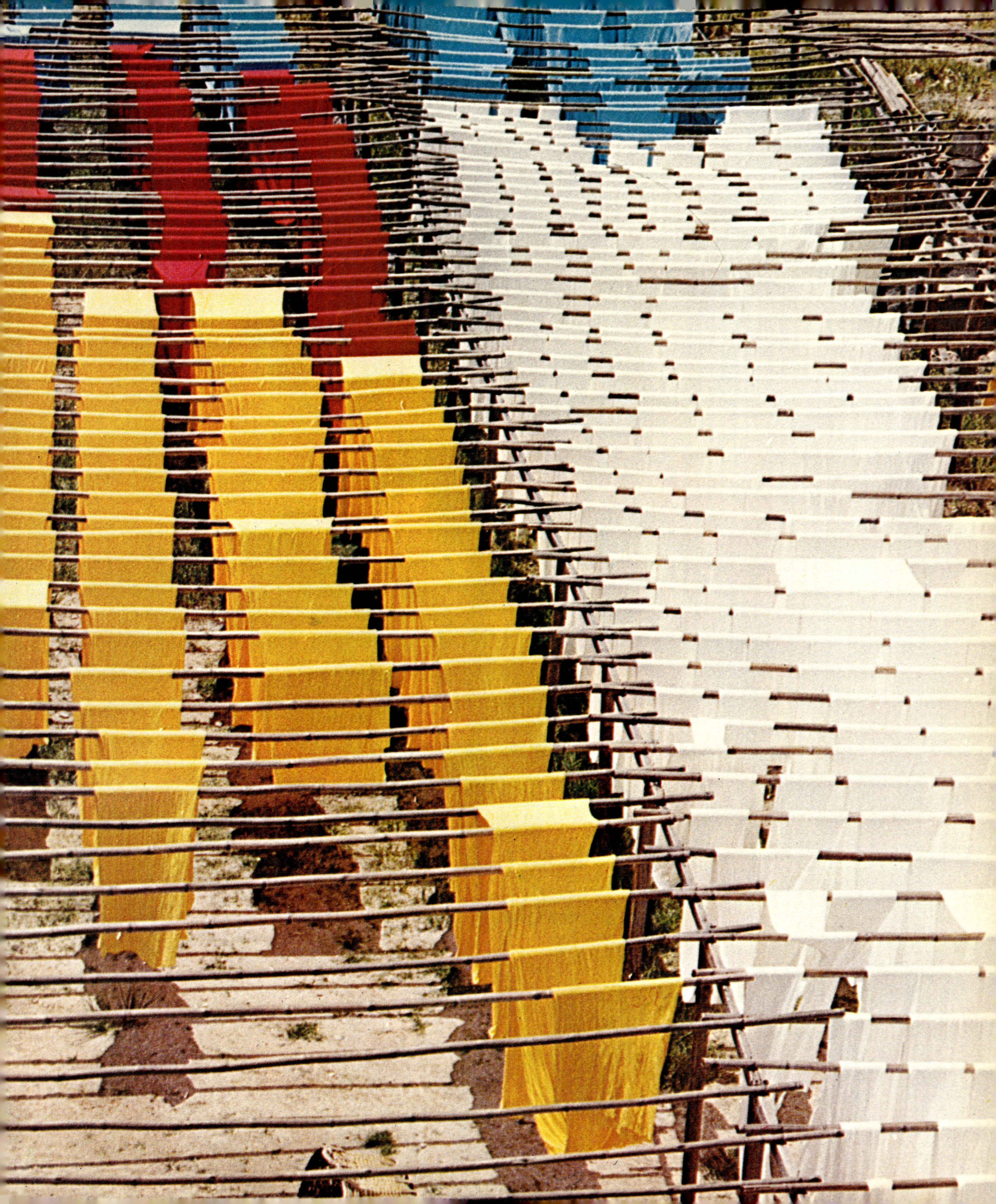

Strip cultivation in the Sha Tau Kok area, where water is precious. Every inch of the land is used.

The restricted border area of Sha Tau Kok between China and Hong Kong.